PLANT ALERT

A GARDEN GUIDE FOR PARENTS

PLANT ALERT

A GARDEN GUIDE FOR PARENTS

CATHERINE COLLINS

Guild of Master Craftsman Publications Ltd

To Walter and Helen.
For your encouragement and support,
I am eternally grateful. C.

First published 2001 by
Guild of Master Craftsman Publications Ltd
166 High Street, Lewes, East Sussex, BN7 1XU

Text © Catherine Collins
© in the Work GMC Publications Ltd

Photographic credits on page 149

ISBN 1 86108 208 8

British Cataloguing in Publication Data.
A catalogue record of this book is available from the British Library.

Cover design by Rob Wheele of Wheelhouse Design
Book design by John Hawkins
Typeset in Caslon

Colour separation by Viscan Graphics Pte Ltd (Singapore)
Printed in Hong Kong by H & Y Printing Ltd

CONTENTS

ABOUT THIS BOOK

The aim of this book is not to scare people away from the plants featured, but to alert parents, teachers and other carers to the potential danger posed by some plants found around the home, in gardens, or on walks in the countryside.

All the plants included have been reported as causing one or more undesirable symptoms in humans. These symptoms are listed and are, for the most part, the worst possible scenario that could occur. However, not everyone will exhibit symptoms, whereas others may develop additional symptoms not listed. This can be due to varying metabolism in the body, medication being taken, or the varying degree of toxicity exhibited by the plant.

This book describes and illustrates the most common plants in the UK that will cause a reaction in humans if eaten or handled. There is limited technical jargon and plants are listed by common name. However, it is important to note that common names have developed from local usage and the same plant may have different common names depending on the locality. Similarly, the same common name may be applied to different plants, so the botanical names are listed as well, to prevent any confusion.

Each plant carries an easy-to-read description, a note of which parts of the plant are poisonous and the symptoms or effects that the plant may cause. Other poisonous plants, less common than those listed in the directory, or which carry only an insignificant risk, are listed separately. There may well be further plants, not reported or listed, which could cause a health risk when in contact with humans, so be vigilant.

Toadstools and fungi are not included, as this is a specialized area and it is safer to stay away from toadstools altogether.

INTRODUCTION

When I allow my pet rabbit the freedom of my garden, I am amazed at his ability to select plants that he has never been offered before, and to eat them without any harm to himself. All manner of plants are eaten, including my prize specimens, but his natural instincts tell which ones to avoid. It is highly likely that when early man was roaming the earth, he also had this instinctive knowledge about which plants to avoid. The need to rely upon wild fruits and berries has been replaced by convenience foods and supermarkets. So aside from tribespeople in remote parts of the world, if humans ever had this ability, it has certainly been lost over the years, leaving us at the mercy of nature.

Fortunately, as we mature we do (hopefully) develop common sense which enables us to steer away from dangerous plants. This learning to survive usually begins with stinging nettles. Once described as needing no description as they can be found on the darkest night, they are a perfect example of how recognition can be instilled into even young children about touching this plant. As a result all similar-looking plants, including the harmless dead-nettle, are usually avoided as well.

Unfortunately learning about other plants to avoid is not that simple. Children love playing outside and gardens can provide a safe and natural environment for them to play in, away from cars and roads. Yet hidden in these havens are trees, shrubs, perennials and other plants which, when in contact with people and especially children, can cause reactions ranging from slight skin irritation to violent skin blisters and mild nausea to vomiting and even death. While household chemicals such as bleach, and medicines and pills come with child-resistant caps, plants are there with no protection from enquiring fingers and mouths. Fatal accidents are, however, few and far between.

Not everyone loves gardening and not everyone has a vast knowledge of plants, but it is important to be aware of those plants which could cause problems if eaten or touched. By teaching children at an early age not to pick and eat any plant without checking with an adult first, most accidents can be avoided. Never take a chance on any fruits, berries or leaves gathered from the wild or the garden unless you are absolutely certain of their identity. Identify all house plants in the home and remove any toxic plants completely, or keep them out of the reach of children and pets. This strategy is common sense. However, as we all know only too well, children will be children and accidents do happen. It is unfortunate also, that many harmful plants in this book have brightly coloured berries to attract children or familiar-looking pods or bulbs which can easily be confused with other non-toxic plants. So by learning more about those particular plants which could cause problems, accidents can be avoided.

WHY ARE PLANTS POISONOUS?

All of the plants included in this book have some kind of adverse effect on humans, whether through contact or ingestion. But why should plants go to such extreme measures to inflict pain and misery on us? The answer in a word is protection. Animals, birds and insects can run, fly and crawl away from danger but plants need something different. While some plants, such as cacti, have developed spines to avoid becoming a quick snack, others have developed chemical protection which has evolved over thousands of years. These chemicals, contained within the plant, have been slowly discovered by man and put to use in medicinal treatments as well as less desirable work.

It is important to realize, too, that most of the essential oils used in aromatherapy and massage are extremely toxic – they are concentrated extracts of the plant and should be kept out of the reach of children.

PLANT FAMILIES

To many people, the use of plant family names is for botanists only and has no significance in everyday life. Many of us are aware of the different family groups such as the onion family containing not only onions but also leeks, chives and garlic. Some families are very easy to recognize due to features common to all members; the pea family, leguminosae (fabaceae) is an example of this: all members of this family have the same shaped flowers and a pod as a seed capsule.

Family members may also share other characteristics, such as chemicals in the plant which have a toxic effect on humans and animals. For this reason I have included the family name with the description of each plant and you will see that plants from particular families predominate. The solanaceae family is one such group, containing such diverse plants as deadly nightshade, tomato, potato, tobacco plant and petunia.

Leguminosae
The pea family make up the second largest family in the plant world with over 500 genera, and are valuable both to the gardener and to the cook. The roots are well-known by gardeners to possess nitrogen-fixing nodules which allow the plant to absorb nitrogen from the air to store in the roots. This ability to replenish a key soil nutrient is why plants from this family form an important part of crop rotation.

In the kitchen, peas, beans and lentils provide essential fibre and protein, particularly useful for vegetarians. Unfortunately they also contain gas-inducing substances which cause flatulence, nausea, cramps and diarrhoea.

Pulses must be well soaked in water and cooked prior to eating to destroy anti-nutritional proteins which can cause these symptoms. The toxins need to be boiled rapidly for ten minutes to be destroyed. Long slow cooking does not destroy the poison.

Solanaceae

This family contains 85 genera, four of which are indigenous to Britain: datura, solanum, atropa and hyoscyamus. The potato, tomato, tobacco plant, petunia and Jerusalem cherry all belong to this family. Some of the most important chemicals found by man are obtained from these family members, including atropine. This is a poisonous alkaloid from deadly nightshade (*Atropa belladonna*), used medicinally to treat peptic ulcers, biliary and renal colic, and as an emergency first-aid counter to exposure to chemical warfare nerve agents, and nicotine (from *Nicotiana tabacum*).

FIRST AID

Poisoning

Any case of suspected poisoning, whether by plant or household substance, requires immediate medical attention. Poisoning due to plant ingestion is uncommon but occurs more often in children who, due to their small body size and susceptibility to toxins, are at greater risk. Children are quite happy playing in the garden and will make up games based on grown-up activities such as cooking. These games can involve collecting nuts, berries, leaves and so on from the garden and making 'pies' and 'puddings'; problems can arise if the food is eaten without the knowledge of a supervising adult.

Symptoms may appear rapidly, or may develop slowly, only becoming apparent later in the day. If you suspect a child has eaten any plant or parts of a plant, e.g. berries, always treat it as an emergency and request medical assistance. Even if the only symptom is vomiting, always seek medical attention as the child may develop other symptoms later. Always try to take a sample of the plant to the hospital or doctors as this will aid recognition and clarify any subsequent treatment required.

- Do not panic
- Do not try to make the person sick, as this may cause additional distress and cause damage internally
- Note time of eating and symptoms
- Take the person to the doctor or casualty department immediately or telephone for an ambulance
- Take a sample of the suspected plant to the doctor or hospital to ensure accurate identification

Skin/Eye Irritation

Many plants will cause redness, irritation and dermatitis on contact with the skin. Other plants may cause a severe reaction such as blisters across the affected part of the body. Blisters are the body's way of protecting the new skin below the damaged part and should never be burst or broken as this will increase the likelihood of infection. Always seek medical attention if there are large areas of affected skin or severe blistering. Always seek medical attention if it is thought that the child may have eaten some of the plant as well.

- Wash the affected area with clean water and seek medical advice
- If the eyes are affected, flush immediately under a cold water tap, for at least 15 minutes. Do not use an eye cup. Treat as an emergency
- If a blister bursts or the skin is broken, sore or swollen, cover with a clean dry gauze dressing and seek medical attention
- Always take a sample of the suspected plant when visiting the doctor or hospital

 This symbol has been used to identify those plants most likely to cause severe illness, as well as death, in children.

THE PLANT DIRECTORY

House
plants
and
tender
perennials

Aloe

Botanical name	*Aloe* spp.
Family name	Liliaceae
Description	Succulent-type house plants with rosettes of thick, fleshy leaves and orange tubular flowers. Best grown in dry air rather than moist
	See also *autumn crocus, bluebell, crown imperial, glory lily, hyacinth, lily-of-the-valley, snake's head fritillary, solomon's seal*

Hazardous part	**All**
Symptoms	**Severe diarrhoea and stomach pains can result if the juice, which is a violent purgative, is ingested**
	In large doses it can cause dehydration and weight loss due to excessive loss of fluid from diarrhoea

Blood lily

Botanical name	*Haemanthus* spp.
Family name	Amaryllidaceae
Description	Tender evergreen house plant, grown from bulbs, which produces a dense head of red star-shaped flowers on tall straight stems
	See also *belladonna lily, cape lily, daffodil, hippeastrum, snowdrop, tulip*
Hazardous part	Bulbs
Symptoms	**Vomiting and diarrhoea if the bulbs are ingested** **Not considered dangerous**

Caladium

Botanical name	*Caladium* spp.
Family name	Araceae
Description	An attractive house plant grown for its colourful heart-shaped leaves which may be patterned green, white, pink or red
	See also *dumb cane, lords and ladies, skunk cabbage*

Hazardous part	**Sap**
Symptoms	**Skin rash may result from contact with this plant, or blistering in severe cases**
	If the plant is ingested it will cause swelling of the mouth and tongue

Cestrum

Botanical name	*Cestrum* spp.
Family name	Solanaceae
Description	A genus of attractive tender shrubs and climbers usually found in cool conservatories and sheltered gardens. The flowers are red, pink or yellow depending on the variety, and are tubular in shape. Red berries follow the flowers

See also *deadly nightshade, henbane, Jerusalem cherry, peppers, potato, thorn apple, tobacco plant, tomato, woody nightshade*

Hazardous part	**All parts are poisonous, especially the berries**
Symptoms	**Skin irritation, with small blisters in severe cases, from contact with the sap**
	Vomiting, gastroenteritis, weakness and muscle paralysis can result if the berries are eaten

Dumb cane

Botanical name	*Dieffenbachia* spp.
Family name	Araceae
Description	A popular evergreen house plant with attractive variegation on the leaves
	See also *caladium, lords and ladies, skunk cabbage*

Hazardous part	**Sap. Avoid handling the plant**
Symptoms	**Burning and irritation of the tongue and mouth, which in turn can affect swallowing and breathing, but dieffenbachias do not cause severe poisoning**
	The cells contain calcium oxalate which causes swelling of the mouth, breathing difficulties and loss of speech for a few days, hence its name dumb cane

Fairy primrose

Botanical name	*Primula obconica*
Family name	Primulaceae
Description	A perennial plant grown as an indoor annual with pretty pink, white, lilac or blue primrose-type flowers. Flowers appear from early winter to late spring
	See also *cyclamen*

Hazardous part	**Leaves**
Symptoms	**A severe allergic reaction may occur, causing swelling, irritation and soreness, if the leaves come into contact with sensitive skin**

Glory lily

Botanical name	*Gloriosa rothschildiana*
Family name	Liliaceae
Description	An aptly named plant with fantastic vivid scarlet, lily-type flowers edged with yellow. A tender climber from Africa, it requires warm, humid conditions to flourish
	See also *aloe, autumn crocus, bluebell, crown imperial, hyacinth, lily-of-the-valley, snake's head fritillary, solomon's seal*

Hazardous part	**Bulbs (tubers)**
Symptoms	**Sickness and diarrhoea if the tubers are eaten**
	Not considered dangerous

Hippeastrum

Botanical name	*Hippeastrum*
Family name	Amaryllidaceae
Description	A commonly grown house plant with large bulbs and large heads of trumpet-shaped flowers in red, white, pink or variations thereof. Often given as presents in boxes ready for growing
	See also *belladonna lily, blood lily, cape lily, daffodil, snowdrop, tulip*

Hazardous part	**Bulb**
Symptoms	**Vomiting and gastroenteritis can result, if the bulb is eaten**

Jerusalem cherry

Botanical name	*Solanum* spp.
Family name	Solanaceae
Description	Both *S. capsicastrum* and *S. pseudocapsicum* are popular house plants, grown for their attractive fruits, which are produced throughout the winter
	See also *cestrum, deadly nightshade, henbane, peppers, potato, thorn apple, tobacco plant, tomato, woody nightshade*

Hazardous part	**Fruits, which are poisonous**
Symptoms	**Abdominal pain and vomiting caused by eating the fruits**
	Skin rashes from contact with the sap

Poinsettia

Botanical name	*Euphorbia pulcherrima*
Family name	Euphorbiaceae
Description	Popular house plant, particularly at Christmas. The upper leaves form white, pink or red bracts which are very attractive
	See also *castor oil plant, dog's mercury, euphorbia*

Hazardous part	**Sap, which is poisonous**
Symptoms	**Blistering of the skin caused by contact with the sap**
	Vomiting, diarrhoea and delirium caused by ingestion of the sap

Trees and
shrubs

Alder buckthorn/black dogwood

Botanical Name	*Frangula alnus*
Family Name	Rhamnaceae
Description	A bushy shrub growing up to, and sometimes beyond, 5.2m (15ft). Usually found on lime soils and heathland. Red berries appear in the autumn and turn black as they ripen
	See also *purging blackthorn*

Hazardous part	**Berries, which resemble sloes, are poisonous and dangerous to children. However, poisoning is uncommon as the fruits contain an extremely bitter juice**
Symptoms	**Violent diarrhoea and physical collapse can result from ingestion of the berries**
	In the past, a syrup was made from the berries and used as a purgative, but this remedy fell out of use as its effects were so violent. Loses its effect when berries are dried

Beech

Botanical name	*Fagus sylvatica*
Family name	Fagaceae
Description	A large tree growing up to 42.6m (140ft) found growing mainly on chalk. The flowers are inconspicuous. The fruits are a triangular nut enclosed in a husk See also *English oak*

Hazardous part	Nuts. Although they are sometimes described as 'edible' they contain toxic substances and, if more than a few are eaten, may produce the symptoms described
Symptoms	Acute abdominal pain, delirium, convulsions and death from asphyxia if eaten in large quantities, but fewer than 50 nuts can cause severe migraine

Bitter almond

Botanical name	*Prunus dulcis*
Family name	Rosaceae
Description	Attractive tree, grown for pretty pink blossom in spring, which appears on bare branches before the leaves
	See also *apricot, hawthorn, laurel*

Hazardous part	Nuts, but they are extremely bitter, discouraging all but the determined from eating them
Symptoms	Vomiting and convulsions can result from ingestion
	Three nuts can kill a child
	The nuts contain a substance known as 'amygdalin' cyanogenic glycoside which, in certain circumstances, can produce prussic acid (hydrogen cyanide)

Box

Botanical name	*Buxus sempervirens*
Family name	Buxaceae
Description	Evergreen shrub/tree found wild only in southern England although commonly used in gardens for low hedging and topiary

Hazardous part	**Roots and leaves**
Symptoms	**Narcotic and sedative effect if juice from the poisonous roots or leaves is ingested**
	Poisoning highly unlikely

Broom

Botanical name	*Cytisus scoparius*
Family name	Leguminosae
Description	A common plant, both in the garden and the wild. Yellow pea-like flowers appear in early summer followed by small pods containing seeds. Differs from gorse as the stems are smooth, rather than prickly. Cultivated forms have different-coloured flowers
	See also *laburnum, lupin, sweet pea, wisteria*

Hazardous part	Seeds
Symptoms	Slowing of the heart rate and vomiting caused by ingestion of the seeds
	Not considered a danger as large quantities are required before any problems occur

Calico bush

Botanical name	*Kalmia latifolia*
Family name	Ericaceae
Description	Evergreen bush with small oval leaves, similar to rhododendron, and attractive pink flowers shaped like parasols. Flowers appear in summer. Needs acid soil
	See also *rhododendron*

Hazardous part	**Leaves and flowers**
Symptoms	**Vomiting and stomach cramps caused by ingestion of the plant**
	Human death has been reported

Elder

Botanical name	*Sambucus nigra*
Family name	Caprifoliaceae
Description	The wild form grows in hedges and on wasteland. Cultivated forms are grown for decorative leaves. Creamy-white flowers appear in early summer and dark clusters of berries form in the autumn
	See also *guelder rose, honeysuckle, snowberry*

Hazardous part	**Leaves, roots, sap and berries**
Symptoms	**Violent vomiting and nausea from ingesting the raw or unfermented berries. Laxative effect in raw state**
	Skin irritation caused by contact with the fresh leaves and berries
	As cooking destroys the toxins, elderberries can be used safely in wine and jam

English oak/sessile oak

Botanical name	*Quercus robur/Quercus petraea*
Family name	Fagaceae
Description	Large tree found across the British Isles. Acorns found late autumn and throughout the winter
	See also *beech*

Hazardous part	**Leaves and acorns**
Symptoms	**Stomach pain and diarrhoea as a result of eating acorns**
	Acorns were used during the war as a substitute for coffee. Any toxicity is removed during the roasting process

Eucalyptus/gum tree

Botanical name	*Eucalyptus* spp.
Family name	Myrtaceae
Description	A large, hardy tree, originating from Australia, which is grown for its unusual bark patterns and attractive grey foliage

Hazardous part	**All. Eucalyptus contains an aromatic oil used for inhalation treatments** **This oil is extremely unpleasant to taste and would deter all but the most determined from eating the leaves**
Symptoms	**Nausea, vomiting, burning sensation in mouth and throat, delirium and convulsions if it is ingested**

Guelder rose

Botanical name	*Viburnum opulus*
Family name	Caprifoliaceae
Description	A native shrub commonly grown in gardens for its heavily scented white flowers and attractive red or yellow berries
	See also *elder, honeysuckle, snowberry*

Hazardous part	**Leaves and sap, but most importantly the berries**
Symptoms	**Irritation of the intestine, vomiting, diarrhoea and eventual collapse can result if the berries are eaten**
	Can be fatal

Hawthorn/may

Botanical name	*Crataegus monogyna*
Family name	Rosaceae
Description	Small tree, commonly used as hedging, which produces creamy-white flowers in spring and red berries in autumn
	See also *apricot, bitter almond, laurel*

Hazardous part	Berries
Symptoms	Stomach cramps, vomiting and diarrhoea if the berries are eaten in large quantities
	Not considered dangerous

Holly

Botanical name	*Ilex aquifolium*
Family name	Aquifoliaceae
Description	Popular shrub or tree grown for decorative berries and for hedging purposes. Found growing wild throughout the British Isles

Hazardous part	**Brightly-coloured berries, which attract children, are poisonous and can be fatal. Do not use real holly on Christmas puddings**
Symptoms	**Vomiting and violent diarrhoea if the berries are ingested**

Horse chestnut

Botanical name	*Aesculus hippocastanum*
Family name	Hippocastanaceae
Description	Large tree found mainly in parks and roadsides with pink or white 'candle' flowers and hard brown nuts used in the game of conkers

Hazardous part	**Nuts or conkers. However they carry only a slight risk of poisoning as they are extremely hard and unappetizing**
Symptoms	**Stomach pains and sickness can result from ingestion. Not thought to be dangerous**

Juniper

Botanical name	*Juniperus communis*
Family name	Cupressaceae
Description	Native evergreen conifer found cultivated in gardens. Grey-blue spiky foliage and cones. The berries are used as a flavouring for gin

Hazardous part	**Leaves**
Symptoms	**The foliage is very prickly and when brushed against skin can produce an itchy painful rash which fades after a few hours**

Laburnum

Botanical name	*Laburnum* spp.
Family name	Leguminosae/Fabaceae
Description	Popular tree found in parks and gardens. Golden yellow flowers appear in late spring/early summer followed by pea-like pods containing up to eight hard brown seeds
	See also *broom, lupin, sweet pea, wisteria*

Hazardous part	All parts are poisonous, but especially the seeds and the bark. The seeds are highly dangerous as they can be mistaken for peas by children. As few as 15 can be fatal to children
Symptoms	Vomiting, stomach cramps, convulsions, coma and death from respiratory failure
	Also dangerous to pets and livestock and has been known to kill horses

Laurel

Botanical name	*Prunus laurocerasus*
Family name	Rosaceae
Description	An evergreen shrub popularly used for hedging and screening. It has oblong, glossy, bright green leaves and white flowers in mid- to late spring. These are followed in late summer by cherry-shaped fruits which turn from red to black
	See also *apricot, bitter almond, hawthorn*

Hazardous part	**All parts are poisonous, especially the leaves and the kernels of the fruit** **Leaves contain hydrocyanic acid which was used by insect collectors as both a means of killing and relaxing specimens**
Symptoms	**Convulsions and respiratory distress may be seen, although death can occur without symptoms**

Mistletoe

Botanical name	*Viscum album*
Family name	Loranthaceae
Description	A perennial evergreen parasitic plant found especially in apple trees. The flowers are inconspicuous but the white berries and leaves are used for Christmas decoration

Hazardous part	**Berries contain a poison known as viscotoxin and are extremely poisonous. When brought inside, the leaves and berries drop very easily. It is important to make sure that any dropped berries are cleared away before they can be picked up by children**
Symptoms	**Gastroenteritis with symptoms such as vomiting and diarrhoea, if the berries are eaten in large quantities. Can be fatal**

Privet

Botanical name	*Ligustrum* spp.
Family name	Oleaceae
Description	A commonly grown shrub used for hedging. *L. vulgare* occurs as a native shrub in woodland edges and in scrub land. Heavily scented white flowers appear in late spring, followed by small black berries in the autumn

Hazardous part	Berries, which are poisonous
Symptoms	Severe gastroenteritis can result, if the berries are eaten. Reports of children being poisoned are rare

Purging buckthorn

Botanical name	*Rhamnus catharticus*
Family name	Rhamnaceae
Description	A large shrub found mainly on chalky soils in southern England. The shrubs have sharp thorns and separate male and female flowers, followed by berries which are green when unripe, but turn black as they ripen. Resembles *Prunus spinosa* (sloe), which is not harmful
	See also *alder buckthorn, black dogwood*

Hazardous part	**Berries**
Symptoms	**Laxative effect if eaten – large doses have an inflammatory effect on bowel leading to nausea and vomiting**
	Dangerous to children

Rhododendron

Botanical name	*Rhododendron* spp.
Family name	Ericaceae
Description	Common evergreen shrub naturalized on acid soil. Purple flowers appear in spring. Cultivated forms, producing an array of colours, may also be harmful
	See also *calico bush*

Hazardous part	Leaves and flowers
Symptoms	Vomiting and stomach pains if ingested
	Not considered dangerous

Sea buckthorn

Botanical name	*Hippophae rhamnoides*
Family name	Elaeagnaceae
Description	A large, decorative shrub or small tree with spines and thin silvery leaves. Bright orange berries appear in autumn and stay on the plant all winter

Hazardous part	**Berries**
Symptoms	**Violent diarrhoea and sickness if the berries are eaten**
	The berries contain a highly bitter-tasting juice which makes them unpopular both with birds and children

Snowberry

Botanical name	*Symphoricarpus albus*
Family name	Caprifoliaceae
Description	Suckering shrubs which are grown in gardens for hedging and for the pink or white fruits which appear during autumn and winter
	See also *elder, guelder rose, honeysuckle*

Hazardous part	Berries, which are poisonous
Symptoms	Skin irritation can result from handling the berries
	Gastroenteritis, vomiting and diarrhoea if taken internally
	The symptoms can be severe, so seek professional advice

Spindle tree

Botanical name	*Euonymus europaeus*
Family name	Celastraceae
Description	A large shrub 1.8–3m (6–9ft) high, grown in gardens for both autumn leaf colour and decorative fruit. The bright pink fruits split open to reveal a single orange seed. A native plant, it can be found mainly on chalky soils and on the edge of woodland
Hazardous part	Bark and leaves, but more importantly the brightly coloured fruits, which attract children
Symptoms	Vomiting and diarrhoea occur up to 12 hours after eating the fruits and this can lead to unconsciousness

Yew

Botanical name	*Taxus baccata*
Family name	Taxaceae
Description	Native shrub or tree with dark green, needle-like flattened leaves, found growing wild and commonly planted in graveyards. The female plant has attractive bright red fruits enclosing a hard red seed
	The drug called taxol is derived from the yew tree and is used in the treatment of cancerous tumours to inhibit cell division

Hazardous part	**Seeds and leaves**
Symptoms	**Vomiting, diarrhoea, convulsions and slowing of the heart. The red juicy part of the berry can be safely eaten but this is not recommended as it is the central hard seed which is poisonous**

Climbers

Black bryony

Botanical name	*Tamus communis*
Family name	Discordiaceae
Description	A perennial climber with large, glossy, heart-shaped leaves and no tendrils. Found in hedgerows throughout England, more easily apparent when the red berries are produced in summer

Hazardous part	**Black roots and the berries. The roots are most toxic, so use gloves if digging the plant out**
Symptoms	**Burning and blistering of the mouth and throat, caused by eating the berries. Abdominal pain and diarrhoea follow. May also cause paralysis in children**
	Can be fatal to children
	If you suspect that your child has eaten berries from this plant, give plenty of milk to drink and seek professional advice immediately

Common/red/white bryony

Botanical name	*Bryonia dioica*
Family name	Cucurbitaccae
Description	A perennial climber, found growing in hedgerows and occasionally in gardens. Small, insignificant flowers appear in summer followed by bright red berries. Tendrils and small, ivy-shaped, leaves distinguish it from black bryony

Hazardous part	**Roots and berries are the main source of poison, although the sap contains irritants**
Symptoms	**Vomiting and diarrhoea. Purgative**
	The milky juice can cause irritation to the skin in the form of redness and blisters
	Up to 15 berries can prove fatal to a child and up to 40 for an adult

Honeysuckle

Botanical name	*Lonicera periclymenum*
Family name	Caprifoliaceae
Description	A climbing plant grown in gardens and found in woodlands across the British Isles. The heavily scented flowers appear from late spring to late summer with bright red sticky berries following
	See also *elder, guelder rose, snowberry*

Hazardous part	Berries
Symptoms	Sickness and diarrhoea, caused by eating the berries
	Not thought to be dangerous

Hops

Botanical name	*Humulus lupulus*
Family name	Cannibaceae
Description	A well-known climbing plant used throughout history as a main ingredient in beer and lager production. Attractive green flowers appear on female plants only in summer and these can be dried for winter decoration. Belongs to same family as the cannabis plant (*Cannabis sativa*)
Hazardous part	**Oils in glands at the base of the flowers. These oils are extremely bitter and give beer its bitter flavour**
Symptoms	**Diarrhoea if ingested** **Sedative effect, hence its use in pillows to enhance sleep**

Ivy

Botanical name	*Hedera* spp.
Family name	Araliaceae
Description	A popular climber found both in the wild and cultivated in gardens. The leaves vary from pale yellow through to dark glossy green. The yellowish-green flowers appear in early autumn and the black globular berries follow in late autumn/early winter

Hazardous part	**Leaves and berries**
Symptoms	**Vomiting and diarrhoea, caused by ingestion, can lead to severe dehydration in young children. Poisoning can lead to serious illness**
	Inflammation of the skin can sometimes develop on contact with the leaves

Morning glory

Botanical name	*Ipomoea caerulea*
Family name	Convolvulaceae
Description	A popular annual climbing plant used for pots and patios during the summer. Attractive blue flowers appear, followed by pea-sized seeds

Hazardous part	**Seeds**
Symptoms	**Confusion, nausea, stomach pain. Severe vomiting and diarrhoea if the seeds are eaten by a child** **Fatalities have been recorded**

Old man's beard

Botanical name	*Clematis vitalba*
Family name	Ranunculaceae
Description	A native perennial found in hedgerows throughout England and Wales with tall climbing stems which can reach 18m (60ft). Small flowers are followed by white fluffy seed heads
	Another name for this plant is traveller's joy, which comes from its use by beggars who, arriving at the gates of a city or town, would rub the sap over their feet to cause blisters and sores to look as if they had been walking a long way
	See also *buttercup, columbine, delphinium, hellebore, kingcup, larkspur, lesser celandine, pasque flower, winter aconite, monkshood*
Hazardous part	**Sap**
Symptoms	**Blistering and dermatitis on sensitive skin if it comes into contact with the sap. Caustic. Poisonous if eaten**

Sweet pea

Botanical name	*Lathyrus × odorata*
Family name	Leguminosae (Fabaceae)
Description	A commonly grown climbing plant, highly prized for its sweet-smelling flowers. Small pea-like pods appear after flowering has finished
	See also *broom, laburnum, lupin, wisteria*

Hazardous part	Seeds. Can be mistaken for peas
Symptoms	Vomiting, diarrhoea and, in severe cases, temporary paralysis of muscles caused by eating the seeds
	Seek medical advice

Swiss-cheese plant

Botanical name	*Monstera deliciosa*
Family name	Araceae
Description	Evergreen, woody-stemmed root climber with large-lobed, holed leaves 40–90cm (16–36in) long. Mature plants bear cream spathes, followed by scented fruits
	See also *caladium, dumb cane, lords and ladies, skunk cabbage*

Hazardous part	**All: it contains calcium oxalate crystals, which are toxic**
Symptoms	**Intense irritation to mucous membranes, producing swelling of tongue, lips and palate**

Wisteria

Botanical name	*Wisteria* spp.
Family name	Leguminosae
Description	A commonly grown climber which produces beautiful white or lilac pea-like flowers in early summer
	See also *broom, laburnum, lupin, sweet pea*

Hazardous part	The seeds, which resemble small peas
Symptoms	Vomiting and diarrhoea caused by eating the seeds. If eaten in large quantities, can affect the heart rate
	Not dangerous unless eaten in large quantities

Flowering
plants:
cultivated

Bleeding heart

Botanical name	*Dicentra spectabilis*
Family name	Fumariaceae
Description	Attractive garden plant grown for pretty pink or white flowers which resemble a heart with a tear-drop dripping out of it. Flowers appear late spring to early summer and occasionally again in late summer
Hazardous part	**Sap. Young children are particularly vulnerable if brushing past the plant**
Symptoms	**Blisters or skin irritations caused by contact with the sap. Even slight bruising of the plant can cause soreness and blisters**

Californian poppy

Botanical name	*Eschscholzia californica*
Family name	Papaveraceae
Description	A hardy annual, growing and self-seeding on quite poor soil in dry sunny positions. Colours range through orange and yellow to white and pink
	See also *corn poppy, greater celandine, horned poppy, opium poppy*

Hazardous part	**Sap and seeds**
Symptoms	**Irritation to sensitive skin can result from contact with the sap** **Stomach upset and vomiting if the seeds are eaten in quantity**

Castor-oil plant

Botanical name	*Ricinis communis*
Family name	Euphorbiaceae
Description	Grown as an annual in gardens. Has large, deeply lobed leaves and unusual green and red flowers in summer which are followed by prickly seed pods
	See also *dog's mercury, euphorbia, poinsettia, spurge*
Hazardous part	**Seeds. These are extremely dangerous to humans: two seeds can cause severe reactions, while six to eight seeds can kill an adult and fewer can be fatal for a child**
Symptoms	**Diarrhoea, muscle spasms and vomiting can result from ingestion of seeds**

Columbine

Botanical name	*Aquilegia vulgaris*
Family name	Ranunculaceae
Description	A common perennial plant found in gardens and in its wild form on wasteland. The wild variety has single dark blue flowers but the cultivated forms can be yellow, pink and white
	See also *buttercup, delphinium, hellebore, kingcup, larkspur, lesser celandine, old man's beard, pasque flower, winter aconite*
Hazardous part	**All parts are thought to be toxic. At one time the dried crushed seeds were used to control head lice but this was discontinued after fatalities occurred**
	The seeds are fatal to children if eaten
Symptoms	**Varied and sudden (as with monkshood, which is from the same family): including numbness, paralysis, difficulty in breathing and a weak and irregular pulse. Death occurs suddenly**

Delphinium

Botanical name	*Delphinium alata*
Family name	Ranunculaceae
Description	A popular perennial plant with tall spikes of blue, white or pink flowers appearing in early summer
	See also *buttercup, columbine, hellebore, kingcup, larkspur, lesser celandine, monkshood, old man's beard, pasque flower, winter aconite*

Hazardous part	**Seeds and leaves, if ingested. Particularly dangerous to children as they are more likely to come into contact with the plant and be more affected by it**
Symptoms	**These are varied and sudden (as with monkshood, which is from the same family): including numbness (caused by the leaf contacting the skin), paralysis of limbs, difficulty and irregularity in breathing and a weak and irregular pulse. Death occurs suddenly**

Elecampane

Botanical name	*Inula helenium*
Family name	Asteraceae (Compositae)
Description	A hardy herbaceous perennial, grown in gardens for its attractive yellow daisy-type flowers
	See also *dandelion, globe artichoke, lettuce, ragwort, yarrow*

Hazardous part	Sap
Symptoms	**Allergic reaction causing irritation and rash can result from contact with the leaves and sap**

Hellebore/Christmas rose

Botanical name	*Helleborus* spp.
Family name	Ranunculaceae
Description	Genus of perennials, usually evergreen, grown as attractive winter-flowering plants. The flowers appear from early to late winter and will last throughout the spring
	See also *buttercup, columbine, delphinium, kingcup, larkspur, monkshood, old man's beard, pasque flower, winter aconite*

Hazardous part	**All parts are poisonous**
Symptoms	**Delirium, convulsions and respiratory failure, followed by death, if ingested** **Seek medical advice as soon as possible**

Hydrangea

Botanical name	*Hydrangea macrophylla*
Family name	Hydrangeaceae
Description	A commonly grown garden plant with large heads of papery flowers in shades of blue, pink and red, depending on species and soil conditions

Hazardous part	**All**
Symptoms	**Irritation to the skin caused by contact with the sap**
	Sickness and diarrhoea may be caused by ingestion
	Other symptoms include a feeling of tightness in the chest and giddiness

Larkspur

Botanical name	*Delphinium ajacis*
Family name	Ranunculaceae
Description	Annual plant grown for pretty spikes of flowers similar to the perennial delphinium. Cultivated in gardens
	See also *buttercup, columbine, delphinium, hellebore, kingcup, lesser celandine, monkshood, old man's beard, pasque flower, winter aconite*

Hazardous part	**Seeds and leaves. Seeds are particularly dangerous to children, as they are more likely to be affected by them**
Symptoms	**Varied and sudden (as with monkshood, which is from the same family): including, paralysis, difficulty in breathing and a weak and irregular pulse following ingestion. Death occurs suddenly**
	Numbness and swelling can result from contact with sap

Lupin

Botanical name	*Lupinus* spp.
Family name	Leguminosae (Fabaceae)
Description	This genus includes both annual and perennial plants. Commonly grown in gardens but also found in the wild
	See also *broom, laburnum, sweet pea, wisteria*

Hazardous part	**All parts are poisonous, especially the seeds. Levels of poison vary greatly from year to year and from species to species**
	Especially dangerous to children
Symptoms	**Slowing of the heart and respiratory system caused by ingestion, also stomach pains, diarrhoea and vomiting**

Mezereon

Botanical name	*Daphne mezereum*
Family name	Thymelaceae
Description	Cultivated wild plant, grown for its highly scented winter flowers, either white or pink, which appear on bare branches from February to March. Red berries follow
Hazardous part	**All, especially the berries which, when ripe resemble redcurrants and are attractive to children. Ingestion of the berries can prove fatal**
Symptoms	**Burning and swelling in the mouth and stomach lining following ingestion of the berries. Unconsciousness may follow, then death**

Opium poppy

Botanical name	*Papaver somniferum* subsp. *hortense*
Family name	Papaveraceae
Description	An annual plant growing wild in parts of England but usually cultivated. Pale lilac flowers with dark blotches at the base of the petals
	This subspecies is not the true opium poppy – *Papaver somniferum* – which only grows in warm climates and contains opium derivatives. Plants grown in the UK do not develop these derivatives fully, but ingestion will still cause the symptoms listed to a lesser extent, so they should be treated as poisonous
	See also *Californian poppy, corn poppy, greater celandine, horned poppy*
Hazardous part	**All parts are poisonous but especially the unripe seed capsules**
Symptoms	**Agreeable mental excitement followed by giddiness after ingestion, as with the drug opium. Other symptoms are increased thirst, a deep sleep, pinpoint pupils, slow irregular breathing and a weak pulse. A coma occurs in rare cases**

Pasque flower

Botanical name	*Pulsatilla vulgaris*
Family name	Ranunculaceae
Description	Grows wild in parts of England but also cultivated, mainly as an alpine plant. Feathery foliage and purple bell-shaped flowers appear in spring, followed by fluffy seed heads
	See also *buttercup, columbine, delphinium, hellebore, kingcup, larkspur, lesser celandine, monkshood, old man's beard, winter aconite*
Hazardous part	Sap and leaves
Symptoms	Skin rash and soreness can result if the leaves are touched
	Not considered dangerous

Skunk cabbage

Botanical name	*Lysichiton americanus*
Family name	Araceae
Description	A cultivated plant grown alongside ponds and ditch beds to provide colour from both leaves and flowers. Offensive smell
	See also *caladium, dumb cane, lords and ladies*

Hazardous part	**Sap. The root and leaves are extremely bitter to taste and not likely to be ingested**
Symptoms	**Severe blisters on the skin, itching and inflammation can result from contact with the fresh plant**

Solomon's seal

Botanical name	*Polygonatum* spp.
Family name	Liliaceae
Description	A herbaceous perennial found growing wild in woodlands but also cultivated in gardens. White tubular flowers appear hanging down the centre of the stems. Black berries appear in autumn
	See also *aloe, autumn crocus, bluebell, crown imperial, glory lily, hyacinth, lily-of-the-valley, snake's head fritillary*

Hazardous part	**Berries, which are poisonous, and may be mistaken for blackcurrants**
Symptoms	**Vomiting and diarrhoea if eaten, but not a highly dangerous plant**

Spurge

Botanical name	*Euphorbia* spp.
Family name	Euphorbiaceae
Description	Euphorbias are commonly found, both in the garden and in the wild. All species have bracts which are more showy than the small and insignificant flowers. The bracts can be pale green, dark green, yellow or red and orange
	See also *castor-oil plant, dog's mercury, poinsettia*
Hazardous part	**White sap, a milky-looking fluid known as latex, which is emitted from any wound to the stem or leaf**
Symptoms	**Rashes and blistering of the skin can be caused by burns from the sap**

Tobacco plant

Botanical name	*Nicotiana tabacum*
Family name	Solanaceae
Description	A 1.8m (6ft) annual, cultivated for its highly scented white flowers
	See also *black nightshade, cestrum, deadly nightshade, henbane, Jerusalem cherry, peppers, potato, thorn apple, tomato, woody nightshade*
Hazardous part	**Leaves contain nicotine which is extremely poisonous and easily absorbed into the skin. They are very sticky and unpleasant to touch**
Symptoms	**Fatal, if ingested. Effects similar to hemlock**
	These guidelines relate specifically to *N. tabacum* but other cultivated varieties of the tobacco plant can also cause problems such as skin rashes

Weeds and
wild plants

Black nightshade

Botanical name	*Solanum nigrum*
Family name	Solanaceae
Description	A low-growing annual plant, with an unpleasant smell. Small white flowers, resembling potato flowers, from mid-summer to mid-autumn, followed by round black berries resembling blackcurrants in late autumn
	Solanum nigrum var *guineese* (the garden huckleberry) is not toxic
	See also *cestrum, deadly nightshade, henbane, Jerusalem cherry, peppers, potato, tobacco plant, thorn apple, tomato, woody nightshade*
Hazardous part	**All, but the toxicity levels vary from plant to plant**
Symptoms	**Gastroenteritis, paralysis, constipation and weakness**

Bogbean

Botanical name	*Menyanthes trifoliata*
Family name	Menyanthaceae
Description	A water plant with white pea-type flowers appearing in summer

Hazardous part	All. However, due to its aquatic nature, it is not considered to be of risk
Symptoms	Severe diarrhoea, stomach pain and nausea can result from ingestion

Bracken

Botanical name	*Pteridium aquilinum*
Family name	Polypodiaceae
Description	Commonly found growing in hillsides and woodland. Large fern-like leaves appear in spring which turn brown and dry in autumn

Hazardous part	**All, especially the root. Poisoning is unlikely in humans but may cause problems with animals if used in bedding. Recent concerns have been about the safety of forestry workers during the summer, as there have been links between inhaling the spores produced by the plant and incidences of cancer, so avoid bracken in high summer if possible**
Symptoms	**If ingested by animals, vitamin B1 deficiency and damage to bone marrow. None listed for humans**

Buttercup

Botanical name	*Ranunculus* spp.
Family name	Ranunculaceae
Description	Common golden flowers growing in hedgerows, fields and gardens
	See also *columbine, delphinium, hellebore, kingcup, larkspur, lesser celandine, monkshood, old man's beard, pasque flower, winter aconite*

Hazardous part	**Sap, which contains irritants. Fortunately, buttercups have an acrid burning taste which will deter all but the most determined from eating it**
Symptoms	**Skin rashes and dermatitis can result from contact with the sap and occasionally, if ingested, gastroenteritis**
	Poisoning is rare in man but may occur if buttercups are ingested by children to see if they taste like butter

Comfrey

Botanical name	*Symphytum officinale*
Family name	Boraginaceae
Description	A wild plant with large hairy leaves. Pretty purple flowers in early summer, which are very attractive to bees
	See also *cherry pie*

Hazardous part	**All. Best avoided unless wearing gloves**
Symptoms	**Dermatitis, when skin contacts hairs on the leaves**

Corn poppy/red poppy

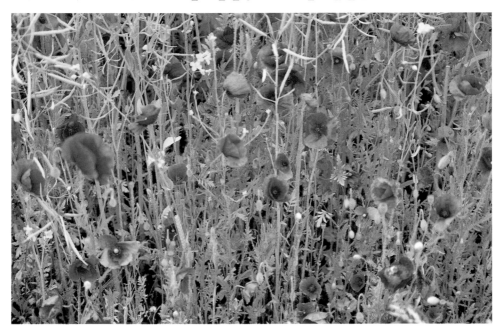

Botanical name	*Papaver rhoeas*
Family name	Papaveraceae
Description	An annual wild plant synonymous with cornfields. Bright red flowers appear in summer
	See also *californian poppy, greater celandine, horned poppy, opium poppy*

Hazardous part	**All**
Symptoms	**If ingested, has a lesser effect than the opium poppy (see page 71) but will still cause drowsiness and irregular breathing**

Couch grass

Botanical name	*Agropyron repens*
Family name	Graminae
Description	An invasive perennial grass in gardens, spreading by underground stems known as rhizomes

Hazardous part	Rhizomes, although it is unlikely that anyone would eat vast quantities of grass roots
Symptoms	Diuretic and sedative if ingested

Dandelion

Botanical name	*Taraxacum officinale*
Family name	Compositae (Asteraceae)
Description	A common weed and wild flower with bright yellow flowers and 'clock' seed heads. Young leaves can be used in salads
	See also *globe artichoke, elecampane, lettuce, ragwort, tansy, yarrow*

Hazardous part	**All, but mainly leaves and root**
Symptoms	**Diuretic effect as well as diarrhoea if too many leaves are eaten**

Deadly nightshade

Botanical name	*Atropa belladonna*
Family name	Solanaceae
Description	A large herbaceous perennial with single dull purple flowers in early summer, followed by single green berries, which change colour through red to black
	See also *black nightshade, cestrum, henbane, Jerusalem cherry, peppers, potato, thorn apple, tobacco plant, tomato, woody nightshade*
Hazardous part	All parts are poisonous and toxin levels increase as the plant matures. It is most toxic in early to mid-summer. The berries are tempting to children: 20–30 are usually fatal, but half a berry has been reported to have killed a child. Death is from respiratory failure
Symptoms	Fatal. Symptoms are flushed dry skin, dilated pupils, dry mouth and delirium

Dog's mercury

Botanical name	*Mercuralis perennis*
Family name	Euphorbiaceae
Description	A commonly found plant used as a chalk soil indicator. Grows in deep shade under trees. The plant, which grows up to 30cm (12in) high, has green spikes of flowers appearing in mid- to late spring
	See also *castor-oil plant, euphorbia, poinsettia*

Hazardous part	**All parts are poisonous. Poisoning has been recorded when leaves were mistaken for a vegetable. Not particularly attractive to children. Previously used as a cure for warts**
Symptoms	**Ingestion causes severe gastric irritation with diarrhoea, nausea and abdominal pain**

Foxglove

Botanical name	*Digitalis purpurea*
Family name	Scrophulariaceae
Description	A genus of biennials and perennials, both wild and cultivated, with large leaves at the base. The tall stems carry white or purple flowers from early to mid-summer. Cultivated forms may vary in colour
Hazardous part	**All parts are poisonous, even when dried, with the poison varying according to growing conditions. Contains digitalin which affects the heart, causing death suddenly**
Symptoms	**Ingestion can cause irritation of the stomach, vomiting and diarrhoea but it is the heart which is most affected, even after a small amount**
	Poisoning is rare, despite the potential danger of the plant. Still used in medicines today

Giant hogweed

Botanical name	*Heracleum mantegazzianum*
Family name	Umbelliferae (Apiaceae)
Description	Huge biennial plant which grows to height of 3–4m (9ft–13ft). Has large white flower heads with an overpowering smell
	See also *angelica, celery, hemlock, parsley, wild parsnip*

Hazardous part	**All**
Symptoms	**On hot sunny days, the hairs on the stems exude oil which causes blisters or painful rash. Children have been scarred around the mouth by using the hollow stems for pea-shooters**
	Ingestion can cause sickness and diarrhoea

Greater celandine

Botanical name	*Chelidonium majus*
Family name	Papaveraceae
Description	A perennial plant found commonly in hedgerows and roadsides. Small yellow, poppy-type flowers appear in early summer
	Can be used externally as a remedy for warts by dabbing sap onto the wart but any juice applied to healthy skin can induce blisters
	See also *californian poppy, corn poppy, horned poppy, opium poppy*

Hazardous part	**All parts are poisonous. The juice is extremely dangerous and it is reported that as little as 50ml (2fl oz) killed a dog**
Symptoms	**Vomiting and diarrhoea if ingested**

Greater plantain

Botanical name	*Plantago major*
Family name	Plantaginaceae
Description	A common weed and wild plant with broad ribbed leaves. Flower spikes are tall and thin and consist of tiny green-black flowers held tightly on the stem

Hazardous part	**Leaves**
Symptoms	**Dermatitis may be caused by contact with the leaves and ingestion has been reported to have a laxative effect**

Hemlock

Botanical name	*Conium maculatum*
Family name	Umbelliferae (Apiaceae)
Description	Large plant growing up to 1.5m (5ft) found on wasteland and meadows in southern England. Very similar to other members of the family but may be distinguished by the irregular purple spots on the stem
	The deadly properties of hemlock have been recognized throughout history
	See also *angelica, celery, giant hogweed, parsley, wild parsnip*

Hazardous part	**All parts are poisonous, especially young leaves and unripe fruit**
Symptoms	**Ingestion causes inflammation of the digestive organs, vomiting and diarrhoea, slow respiration and rapid pulse becoming slower. Paralysis, convulsions and coma follow. Death is from respiratory failure**

Henbane

Botanical name	*Hyocyamus niger*
Family name	Solanaceae
Description	A 90cm (3ft) annual or biennial with yellowish leaves and greenish flowers appearing in mid- to late summer. A green capsule containing several seeds follows in autumn. Grows on wasteland throughout England
	See also *black nightshade, cestrum, Jerusalem cherry, deadly nightshade, peppers, potato, thorn apple, tobacco plant, tomato, woody nightshade*
Hazardous part	**All parts are poisonous. Deaths have been recorded from the root being eaten, in the belief that it was chicory or parsnips but, because of its unpleasant taste, poisoning is rare**
Symptoms	**If ingested, effects are similar to that of deadly nightshade, which is in the same family: flushed dry skin, dilated pupils, dry mouth and delirium**

Herb paris

Botanical name	*Paris quadrifolia*
Family name	Trilliaceae
Description	An unusual low-growing plant with a single stem and four leaves in a rosette formation around the stem. A single green flower appears on top of the stem followed by a small black fruit resembling a blackberry. Found in damp chalky woods

Hazardous part	**All, especially the fruit**
Symptoms	**Severe purging and vomiting. Dangerous to children**

Horned poppy

Botanical name	*Glaucium flavum*
Family name	Papaveraceae
Description	Bright yellow poppy flowers found growing along shingle beaches. The seed pod is very long and twisted
	See also *californian poppy, corn poppy, greater celandine, opium poppy*

Hazardous part	**All**
Symptoms	**Stomach upset as well as a sedative effect, if the plant is ingested Irritation to the skin can be caused by contact with the sap**

Kingcup/marsh marigold

Botanical name	*Caltha palustris*
Family name	Ranunculaceae
Description	A beautiful sight in the spring when bright gold flowers appear. Grows in damp places, both in the wild and cultivated in gardens
	See also *buttercup, columbine, delphinium, hellebore, larkspur, lesser celandine, monkshood, old man's beard, pasque flower, winter aconite*

Hazardous part	Sap
Symptoms	**Dermatitis and small blisters from handling the stems and leaves**

Lesser celandine

Botanical name	*Ranunculus ficaria*
Family name	Ranunculaceae
Description	Bright yellow flowers resembling buttercups with green fleshy leaves. Appears in early and mid-spring
	See also *buttercup, columbine, delphinium, hellebore, kingcup, larkspur, monkshood, old man's beard, pasque flower, winter aconite*

Hazardous part	Sap
Symptoms	**Dermatitis and blistering can be caused by sap on the skin**
	The tubers have been eaten in salads but this is not recommended

Lords and ladies/cuckoo pint

Botanical name	*Arum italicum/Arum maculatum*
Family name	Araceae
Description	A common sight in hedgerows in spring, with a large green flowering spike followed by red berries in the autumn. *A. italicum* is larger than *A. maculatum*, which has spots on the leaves
	See also *caladium, dumb cane, skunk cabbage*
Hazardous part	**Roots and berries. Root also contains a poison which, when cooked, is rendered harmless. All parts produce an acrid burning juice which is a serious irritant both internally and externally**
Symptoms	**Vomiting and diarrhoea if ingested, blistering and redness if in contact with the skin**

Monkshood

Botanical name	*Aconitum napellus*
Family name	Ranunculaceae
Description	A 1.2m (4ft) herbaceous perennial with bright green divided leaves and attractive dark blue flowers. Found in gardens and in the wild
	See also *buttercup, columbine, delphinium, hellebore, kingcup, larkspur, lesser celandine, old man's beard, pasque flower, winter aconite*
Hazardous part	**All parts are poisonous. The root is the most dangerous and maximum toxicity is reached in the leaves just before flowering**
	Monkshood is fatal to man. Reportedly the most dangerous of British plants
Symptoms	**Varied and sudden. They include numbness, paralysis, difficulty in breathing and a weak and irregular pulse. Death occurs suddenly**
	Hospitalize immediately

Stinging nettle

Botanical name	*Urtica dioica*
Family name	Urticaceae
Description	Two types of nettle, the perennial and the annual variety can both be found on wasteland, cultivated ground and roadsides. The flowers are green and insignificant as opposed to the harmless dead-nettle which has large white flowers
	Dock, rhubarb, rosemary, mint and sage leaves will sooth the rash caused by contact
	The acid in stinging nettle is destroyed by cooking and it can be used as a vegetable, served like cabbage
Hazardous part	**Serrated leaves with stinging hairs and stems. The stinging nettle contains formic acid and ammonia although its sap is an antidote to itself. The hairs are hollow and the basal cells emit juice**
Symptoms	**Stinging sensation and rash**

Ragwort

Botanical name	*Senecio jacobaea*
Family name	Compositae/Asteraceae
Description	A native plant, usually perennial, which is common on waste ground, farmland and roadsides. The bright yellow flowers, which appear during the summer, attract the cinnabar moth with its distinctive yellow and black striped caterpillars. These caterpillars are able to absorb the poisonous proteins from the plant, so making themselves undesirable to predators
	See also *dandelion, elecampane, globe artichoke, lettuce, tansy, yarrow*

Hazardous part	**All**
Symptoms	**Skin rash can be caused by the sap**
	Vomiting may occur if eaten, but it is unlikely to be ingested by humans as it is not attractive in flavour or smell

Rough chervil

Botanical name	*Chaerophyllum temulentum*
Family name	Umbelliferae (Apiaceae)
Description	A plant found growing on roadsides and woodland edges, growing up to 80cm (32in) tall. White flowers in summer and late autumn. Very similar to hemlock in appearance, but smaller, with redness leading up to the leaf bracts rather than the spotted stems which are typical of hemlock
	See also *angelica, celery, giant hogweed, hemlock, parsley, wild parsnip*
Hazardous part	**All**
Symptoms	**Sickness, giddiness and vomiting caused by ingestion**

St John's wort

Botanical name	*Hypericum perforata*
Family name	Guttiferae
Description	A common perennial with small bright yellow flowers which appear in summer. Used in herbal remedies. Other species are grown in gardens

Hazardous part	**Sap, which is photo-sensitive**
Symptoms	**Rash or blisters on skin, if the sap is in contact with skin in sunlight**
	Other species of hypericum may also cause lesser symptoms

Shepherd's purse

Botanical name	*Capsella bursa-pastoris*
Family name	Cruciferae
Description	A common garden weed with tiny white flowers and heart-shaped seed pods
	See also *horseradish*

Hazardous part	**All**
Symptoms	**Breathing problems, sedation and mild paralysis can result from ingesting excessive amounts of shepherd's purse**

Spurge laurel

Botanical name	*Daphne laureola*
Family name	Thymelaceae
Description	A native perennial plant found mainly in England but introduced elsewhere. Grows to a height of 90cm (3ft). The leaves tend to be confined to the end of the branches. Small green flowers appear in summer followed by rubbery berries
Hazardous part	**Berries**
Symptoms	**Vomiting and diarrhoea can result from ingestion, particularly in small children** **Not considered a dangerous plant**

Stinking iris

Botanical name	*Iris foetidissima*
Family name	Iridaceae
Description	A popular perennial plant found in gardens and woods. Violet-blue flowers are produced in early summer followed by bright orange seeds in autumn which remain throughout the winter
	During the sixteenth century, the plant was infused into tea and beer to provide a 'purging' effect
	See also *gladioli, yellow flag*

Hazardous part	All parts are thought to be poisonous but it is the bright berries which attract children. The whole plant is poisonous to pets
Symptoms	Stomach cramps and diarrhoea can result if the berries are eaten

Tansy

Botanical name	*Tanacetum vulgare*
Family name	Compositae (Asteraceae)
Description	A wild plant cultivated in the herb garden with yellow flowers appearing in late summer. Leaves have an unusual fragrance when crushed
	See also *dandelion, elecampane, globe artichoke, lettuce, ragwort, yarrow*

Hazardous part	**All. The oil from the plant is poisonous**
Symptoms	**Pulse irregularity, severe diarrhoea and convulsions can result from ingesting the plant**
	Allergic reaction may result if the sap is in contact with the skin

Thorn apple

Botanical name	*Datura stramonium*
Family name	Solanaceae
Description	A 91cm (3ft) annual found on common and cultivated ground. Single white or violet flowers are followed by a prickly capsule containing several seeds. Also cultivated as a house plant
	See also *black nightshade, cestrum, deadly nightshade, henbane, Jerusalem cherry, peppers, potato, thorn apple, tobacco plant, tomato, woody nightshade*
Hazardous part	**Leaves and unripe capsules but especially the seeds. Children, who can be attracted to the unusual seed capsules, are particularly at risk and the half-ripe seeds have an attractive sweet flavour which does not discourage them. The poison is not destroyed by boiling or drying**
Symptoms	**Fatalities have been reported. The symptoms are similar to that of deadly nightshade, which is in the same family: flushed, dry skin, dilated pupils, dry mouth and delirium. Juice in the eyes makes the pupils dilate**

Wild parsnip

Botanical name	*Pastinaca sativa*
Family name	Umbelliferae
Description	Commonly found on wasteland in southern England, particularly on chalk. Grows to a height of 60cm–1.2m (2–4ft) and has the aroma of parsnips when crushed
	See also *angelica, celery, giant hogweed, hemlock, parsley*
Hazardous part	Sap
Symptoms	**Blisters and dermatitis can be caused by the sap, particularly with small children**

Wood anemone

Botanical name	*Anemone nemerosa*
Family name	Ranunculaceae
Description	Grows from a corm. Delicate white flowers appear in woodland in spring, usually alongside bluebells. Disappears once flowering has finished
	See also *buttercup, columbine, delphinium, hellebore, kingcup, larkspur, lesser celandine, monkshood, old man's beard, pasque flower, winter aconite*
Hazardous part	**Leaves. Very bitter taste, so deters all but the most determined from eating it. Not considered dangerous**
Symptoms	**Dermatitis and skin rash. Gastroenteritis if eaten in large quantities**

Woody nightshade

Botanical name	*Solanum dulcamara*
Family name	Solanaceae
Description	A climbing or trailing woody perennial, which can grow up to 1.8m (6ft). Attractive purple flowers are followed by bright red berries. Unripe berries have been gathered with peas, as they look very similar

See also *black nightshade, cestrum, deadly nightshade, henbane, Jerusalem cherry, peppers, potato, tobacco plant, thorn apple, tomato*

Hazardous part	**All parts are poisonous. Berries are bitter at first, becoming sweeter. Just six berries can cause paralysis in a child**
Symptoms	**Gastroenteritis, constipation, weakness and paralysis caused by ingestion, with symptoms become more severe, depending on how many berries have been eaten. Poisoning is rarely fatal and children have been known to recover in 24 hours**

Yarrow/milfoil

Botanical name	*Achillea millefolium*
Family name	Compositae (Asteraceae)
Description	A common lawn weed, but also cultivated for its tall pink, white or yellow flower heads
	See also *dandelion, elecampane, globe artichoke, lettuce, ragwort, tansy*

Hazardous part	**All**
Symptoms	**Violent skin reactions can be caused by the sap in the leaves, usually when it gets crushed by someone walking or falling on it. The reaction may be insignificant but occasionally a bad rash can occur**

Yellow flag

Botanical name	*Iris pseudacorus*
Family name	Iridaceae
Description	A common sight along rivers, streams and ponds. A bright yellow flower appears in late spring to early summer, followed by a brown seed capsule
	See also *gladioli, stinking iris*

Hazardous part	Leaves and root, but ingestion is rare due to the extremely bitter taste
Symptoms	Gastroenteritis, i.e. vomiting and diarrhoea, can result from ingestion
	Not considered dangerous

Bulbs

Autumn crocus

Botanical name	*Colchicum autumnale*
Family name	Liliaceae
Description	Large pink or white crocus-type flowers appear from early to late autumn, with large flat leaves appearing after the flowers
	C. autumnale is named after Colchis on the Black Sea, where the plant is found wild. Contains colchicine, an alkaloid used in genetic engineering to double the chromosomes in a cell
	See also *aloe, bluebell, crown imperial, glory lily, hyacinth, lily-of-the-valley, snake's head fritillary, Solomon's seal*

Hazardous part	**Bulbs**
Symptoms	**May cause sickness and vomiting if ingested**

Bluebell

Botanical name	*Hyacinthoides non-scriptus*
Family name	Liliaceae
Description	A common woodland plant, with blue, white or pink flowers. There is also a larger, cultivated form. The bulbs are smooth and white and the size of grapes. They are often found on the surface of the soil
	See also *aloe, autumn crocus, crown imperial, glory lily, hyacinth, lily of the valley, snake's head fritillary, Solomon's seal*

Hazardous part	**Bulbs, which are are poisonous**
Symptoms	**Abdominal pain, diarrhoea and a slow, weak pulse. In large doses, vomiting occurs**
	Poisoning is rare and usually only occurs when the bulbs have been mistaken for onions

Belladonna lily

Botanical name	*Amaryllis belladonna*
Family name	Amaryllidaceae
Description	A beautiful flowering bulb with large pink trumpet-type flowers. Will grow in gardens with protection from cold and wet, so ideal in a south or west position. The flowers may be cut for indoor decoration
	See also *blood lily, cape lily, daffodil, hippeastrum, snowdrop, tulip*

Hazardous part	Bulb
Symptoms	Vomiting, diarrhoea and convulsions can result from ingestion

Cape lily

Botanical name	*Crinum* spp.
Family name	Amaryllidaceae
Description	Beautiful pale pink and white trumpet flowers appear from mid-summer to early autumn. Tender bulbs, they are best planted in a cool conservatory or sheltered spot
	See also *belladonna lily, blood lily, daffodil, hippeastrum, snowdrop, tulip*

Hazardous part	**Bulb**
Symptoms	**The bulb, if eaten, causes vomiting and diarrhoea**

Crown imperial

Botanical name	*Fritillaria imperialis*
Family name	Liliaceae
Description	A spectacular, tall-stemmed, spring-flowering bulb. Has up to five widely bell-shaped flowers around the top, crowned by small leaf-like bracts and a very distinctive aroma of cats
	See also *aloe, autumn crocus, bluebell, glory lily, hyacinth, lily-of-the-valley, snake's head fritillary, Solomon's seal*
Hazardous part	**Bulb**
Symptoms	**The bulb, if eaten, can cause sickness and diarrhoea. It can also have a slowing effect on the heart, but only if eaten in large amounts**

Cyclamen

Botanical name	*Cyclamen hederifolium*
Family name	Primulaceae
Description	Pretty pink and white flowers appear in early to mid-autumn. Very hardy and grown in gardens in shady places
	See also *fairy primrose*

Hazardous part	Sap
Symptoms	**Skin irritation and soreness can result if handled without gloves. Not considered dangerous**

Daffodil

Botanical name	*Narcissus* spp.
Family name	Amaryllidaceae
Description	Common spring flower with heads of yellow, white or orange
	See also *belladonna lily, blood lily, cape lily, hippeastrum, snowdrop, tulip*

Hazardous part	**Bulbs. Store away from children – can be mistaken for onions**
Symptoms	**Severe vomiting, diarrhoea and convulsions may result if the bulb is eaten**

Gladioli

Botanical name	*Gladiolus* spp.
Family name	Iridaceae
Description	A commonly grown garden plant with tall spikes of brightly coloured flowers which make excellent cut flowers. Smaller flowering species are also cultivated
	See also *stinking iris, yellow flag*

Hazardous part	**Bulbs (corms)**
Symptoms	**Ingestion can cause diarrhoea and vomiting, but not considered dangerous**

Hyacinth

Botanical name	*Hyacinthus* spp.
Family name	Liliaceae
Description	Genus of bulbs, commonly grown for spring colour and fragrance. Flowers may be blue, pink, red, white, yellow or orange
	See also *aloe, autumn crocus, bluebell, crown imperial, glory lily, lily-of-the-valley, snake's head fritillary, Solomon's seal*

Hazardous part	**Bulb. Handling the bulb with sensitive skin can produce an unpleasant rash and dermatitis**
Symptoms	**If eaten, the bulbs can cause severe vomiting and sickness**

Lily-of-the-valley

Botanical name	*Convallaria majalis*
Family name	Liliaceae
Description	Commonly grown spring-flowering perennial with sweetly scented white flowers followed by red berries in the autumn
	See also *aloe, autumn crocus, bluebell, crown imperial, glory lily, hyacinth, snake's head fritillary, Solomon's seal*
Hazardous part	Whole plant, which is poisonous. Although the flowers are said to be more dangerous, it is the berries which attract children
Symptoms	If ingested, the cardioglycosides act on the heart causing slow, irregular pulse, severe abdominal pain, vomiting, dilated pupils, clammy skin, delirium, coma and death. Seek immediate medical attention

Snake's head fritillary

Botanical name	*Fritillaria meleagris*
Family name	Liliaceae
Description	A delicate-looking flower with a chequerboard effect on its petals. Grows wild in very few parts of Britain as it is in decline. Cultivated in gardens and rockeries
	See also *aloe, autumn crocus, bluebell, crown imperial, glory lily, hyacinth, lily-of-the-valley, snake's head fritillary, Solomon's seal*

Hazardous part	**Bulb**
Symptoms	**If eaten, the bulb can cause vomiting and diarrhoea**
	Not usually considered dangerous

Snowdrop

Botanical name	*Galanthus nivalis*
Family name	Amaryllidaceae
Description	A commonly grown winter-flowering bulb which naturalizes easily. Also found in the wild. The white nodding flowers appear in mid-winter along with slender grey-green leaves
	See also *belladonna lily, blood lily, cape lily, daffodil, hippeastrum, tulip*
Hazardous part	**Bulbs contain toxins. The dry bulbs should be stored away from children who may mistake them for onions**
Symptoms	**The bulbs, if eaten, can cause severe gastroenteritis, vomiting, diarrhoea and occasionally convulsions**

Tulip

Botanical name	*Tulipa* spp.
Family name	Amaryllidaceae
Description	A very popular late spring flower with brightly coloured flowers. The bulb is smooth and very similar to the onion, but is reddish brown and has no layers immediately visible
	See also *belladonna lily, blood lily, cape lily, daffodil, hippeastrum, snowdrop*

Hazardous part	Bulb. Similar in appearance to onion bulbs – store away from children
Symptoms	Vomiting and severe diarrhoea can result if the bulb is eaten

Winter aconite

Botanical name	*Eranthis hyemalis*
Family name	Ranunculaceae
Description	Pretty yellow flowers appearing in mid- to late winter. Stems are only 2.5–5cm (1–2in) high. Grows from a corm
	The root was once used to tip arrows to kill wolves and it was grown in medieval times to control vermin, as it was reliable and quick
	See also *buttercup, columbine, delphinium, hellebore, kingcup, lesser celandine, monkshood, old man's beard, pasque flower*

Hazardous part	**All, especially the root. More deadly than prussic acid**
Symptoms	**Poisonous**
	Hospitalize immediately

Herbs

Angelica

Botanical name	*Angelica archangelica*
Family name	Umbelliferae/Apiaceae
Description	A very large garden plant grown in herb gardens mainly as an annual or biennial. The stems are candied and used in cake decoration
	See also *celery, giant hogweed, hemlock, parsley, wild parsnip*

Hazardous part	Sap, if it comes into contact with the skin in sunlight
Symptoms	Irritation and blistering to the skin

Horseradish

Botanical name	*Armoracia rusticana*
Family name	Cruciferae
Description	A large-leaved herbaceous perennial with white roots similar to dandelion roots in appearance, but much thicker
	See also *shepherd's purse*

Hazardous part	**All, especially the root but, in spite of this, the root is used to make horseradish sauce**
Symptoms	**Extremely irritant to both skin and nasal membranes, so it is as well to wear rubber gloves when handling it. Ingestion in large quantities can cause inflammation of the stomach**

Parsley

Botanical name	*Petroselinum crispum*
Family name	Umbelliferae (Apiaceae)
Description	A plant grown as a herb and widely used in cooking
	See also *angelica, celery, giant hogweed, hemlock, wild parsnip*

Hazardous part	**Sap: contact with skin in sunlight may cause a sensitive reaction**
Symptoms	**Irritation and blistering in severe cases**

Pennyroyal

Botanical name	*Mentha pulegium*
Family name	Labiatae
Description	A herb grown in gardens for its attractive flowers and aroma
	See also *thyme*

Hazardous part	**All. Toxic to humans**
Symptoms	**If ingested, causes stomach cramps, nausea, vomiting, diarrhoea, raised blood pressure and pulse, and a nettle-type rash from contact**
	Deaths have been reported

Rue

Botanical name	*Ruta graveolens*
Family name	Rutaceae
Description	Attractive evergreen plant grown for its grey-green leaves and greeny-yellow flowers. The plant has a distinctive aroma when the leaves are crushed and can be used sparingly in salads

Hazardous part	**Leaves and sap**
Symptoms	**Dermatitis from contact with the fresh plant. Allergic skin reaction aggravated by direct sunlight**

Thyme

Botanical name	*Thymus vulgaris*
Family name	Labiatae
Description	A popular herb grown for its culinary uses. Flowers are very attractive to bees
	See also *pennyroyal*

Hazardous part	**All. Thyme oil is poisonous, although small quantities of the plant may be safely used in cookery**
Symptoms	**Ranging from headache, dizziness, nausea, stomach pain, convulsions, cardiac and respiratory problems, if large amounts are eaten, particularly if raw**
	Soreness and inflammation from skin contact

Fruit and vegetables

Apricot

Botanical name	*Prunus armeniaca*
Family name	Rosaceae
Description	A summer fruit, grown mainly abroad as a warm temperature is required. Can be bought fresh from supermarkets and greengrocers
	See also *bitter almond, hawthorn, laurel*
Hazardous part	**Kernel: in its raw state it contains cyanide. The poison is neutralized when the kernels are roasted and traditionally they are used in cooking around the world for their bitter almond taste. However, never eat a raw apricot kernel, as hydrogen cyanide is released once the kernel is eaten**
Symptoms	**Vomiting, diarrhoea and breathlessness can result from ingestion and respiratory failure may follow if these symptoms are left untreated. Fatalities have been reported**

Celery

Botanical name	*Apium graveolens*
Family name	Umbelliferae (Apiaceae)
Description	A common salad vegetable with succulent fleshy stems and slightly hot leaves. Distinctive aroma and taste
	See also *angelica, giant hogweed, hemlock, parsley, wild parsnip*

Hazardous part	Sap
Symptoms	Irritation and blistering can occur if the sap comes into contact with the skin in sunlight
	Allergic reactions to eating celery have also been recorded. Avoid discoloured stems and leaves, as these are more likely to cause problems

Globe artichoke

Botanical name	*Cynara scolymus*
Family name	Compositac (Asteraceae)
Description	A tall thistle-like plant grown in vegetable gardens for the fleshy base of the flower head. Silvery-grey foliage is very attractive and it is often grown in flower borders for its architectural height
	See also *dandelion, elecampane, lettuce, ragwort, tansy, yarrow*

Hazardous part	Sap
Symptoms	**Skin irritation and dermatitis can result from contact with the leaves**

Lettuce

Botanical name	*Lactuca sativa*
Family name	Compositae (Asteraceae)
Description	A common garden vegetable used for salad dishes
	See also *dandelion, elecampane, globe artichoke, ragwort, tansy, yarrow*

Hazardous part	**All, especially the milky sap or latex**
Symptoms	**Irritation to the skin and occasionally an allergic reaction**
	Large quantities of lettuce are reportedly sedative in effect although it would require a large dose

Peppers

Botanical name	*Capsicum* spp.
Family name	Solanaceae
Description	A greenhouse-grown vegetable with green, red or orange fruits with different shapes according to variety. Some have a mild sweet taste, whilst others are extremely hot
	See also *black nightshade, cestrum, deadly nightshade, henbane, Jerusalem cherry, potato, thorn apple, tobacco plant, tomato, woody nightshade*

Hazardous part	**Fruit. Most people have eaten peppers in some form, either raw or cooked, with little or no effect. However, over-indulgence of some varieties, particularly the hot ones, should be avoided**
Symptoms	**Severe gastroenteritis can result and, in extreme cases, kidney failure**
	The oil from the pepper is an irritant to the eyes and nose

Potato

Botanical name	*Solanum tuberosum*
Family name	Solanaceae
Description	Commonly grown vegetable producing large tubers used in cooking. Flowers, which are generally white or pink, appear during the summer, followed by a round green fruit
	See also *black nightshade, cestrum, deadly nightshade, henbane, Jerusalem cherry, peppers, thorn apple, tobacco plant, tomato, woody nightshade*
Hazardous part	**The fruit, which resembles an unripe tomato, and all the other green parts including green tubers. Always throw away green or sprouting potato tubers**
Symptoms	**Stomach cramps, diarrhoea and vomiting caused by ingestion of the fruit and leaves, which contain poisonous glycoalkaloids called solanine and atropine**

Rhubarb

Botanical name	*Rheum × hybridum*
Family name	Polygonaceae
Description	A commonly grown vegetable used for jams, pies, crumbles etc. Large green leaves appear at the end of reddish-pink stalks. Tall white flowers appear in summer

Hazardous part	**Leaf: the leaf blade contains high concentrations of oxalic acid, a chemical compound. The stem is safe to eat, providing the leaf is removed with at least 5cm (2in) of stalk below**
Symptoms	**Oxalic acid ingestion can cause muscle and kidney damage, coma and even death**

Tomato

Botanical name	*Lycopersicum esculentum*
Family name	Solanaceae
Description	An annual plant grown for its tasty red or yellow fruits. Yellow flowers are produced in summer, followed by the edible fruits
	See also *black nightshade, cestrum, deadly nightshade, henbane, Jerusalem cherry, peppers, potato, tobacco plant, woody nightshade*

Hazardous part	**Root, stem and leaves are poisonous. Do not feed animals the leaves or shoots**
Symptoms	**The effects of eating the leaves are similar to those of woody nightshade, which is from the same family: gastroenteritis, constipation, weakness and paralysis**
	The sap from the plant can cause severe irritation if in contact with the skin

OTHER PLANTS WHICH MAY PROVE HAZARDOUS

Apple (*Malus sylvestris*) pips: similar to apricot
Ash (*Fraxinus excelsior*) seeds: stomach pains and vomiting
Aubergine (*Solanum melongena*) sap: skin irritation, similar to tomato (page 147)
Azalea: see rhododendron (page 41)
Baneberry (*Actaea spicata*) berries: increased heart rate, vomiting, dizziness
Berberis (*Berberis* spp.) berries and spines: sickness and diarrhoea, skin irritation
Cherry pie (*Heliotropium × hybridum*) sap: contact may cause skin soreness and irritation
Fool's parsley (*Aethusa cynapium*): all parts. Similar to hemlock (page 92), but less severe
Globe flower (*Trollius europaeus*) sap, similar to buttercup (page 81)
Gorse (*Ulex europaeus*) seeds: see broom (page 26)
Groundsel (*Senecio vulgaris*) sap: similar to ragwort (page 101)
Iceland poppy (*Papaver nudicaule*): all parts. Similar to corn poppy (page 83)
Lantana camara: all parts. Skin irritation and vomiting if ingested
Locust (*Robinia pseudoacacia*) seeds: similar to laburnum (page 36), but less severe
Nerium (*Nerium oleander*) sap: similar to spurge (page 75), but also vomiting and
    diarrhoea if ingested
Oregon grape (*Mahonia* spp.) fruit: can cause stomach pains, if ingested
Philodendron sap: similar to dumb cane (page 14)
Pieris (*Pieris* spp.) spines: rash from contact with the spines
Rowan (*Sorbus aucuparia*) berries: convulsions and breathing problems, if ingested
Soapwort (*Saponaria officinalis*) seeds and sap: breathing irregularities, if ingested
Spring snowflake (*Leucojum vernum*) bulb: similar to snowdrop (page 127)
Summer snowflake (*Leucojum* spp.) bulb: "   "   "   "   "
Virginia creeper (*Parthenocissus* spp.) sap: skin irritation
Wallflower (*Cheiranthus cheiri*) seeds: can cause vomiting if ingested, but not severe
Water lily (*Nymphaea*) sap: skin irritation
Wayfaring tree (*Viburnum lantana*) fruit: vomiting, if ingested
Woad (*Isatis tinctoria*) sap: vomiting, if ingested, but not severe
Wormwood (*Artemesia absinthium*): all parts. Skin irritation
Yellow rattle (*Rhinanthus serotinus*) sap: vomiting and diarrhoea

BIBLIOGRAPHY

The Baby and Child Medical Handbook,
Dr Miriam Stoppard, Dorling Kindersley, London 1986

Food for Free,
Richard Mabey, William Collins, 1972

Garden Plants and Flowers Encyclopedia,
Reader's Digest Association Ltd, London 1978

Horticultural Trade Association, Information Leaflet

The New Oxford Book of Food Plants,
J.G. Vaughan and C.A. Geissler, Oxford University Press, Oxford 1997

Poisonous Plants and Fungi,
Pamela North, Blandford Press, London 1967

The Wild Garden,
Lys de Bray, Weidenfeld & Nicolson, London 1978

Wild Flowers of Britain,
Roger Phillips Pan Books Ltd, London 1977

ACKNOWLEDGEMENTS

Photographs reproduced by kind permission of the copyright holders:

ANTHONY BAILEY, pp. 30, 90 and 128. A–Z BOTANICAL COLLECTION LTD, p. 40. CATHERINE COLLINS, pp. ii, 12–14, 22, 25, 27, 28 (r), 29, 32, 36 (r), 42, 44, 46–8, 50–3, 54 (l), 55, 60, 62, 64 (r), 66–7, 69 (r), 73–7, 83, 87, 89, 91, 99 (x 2), 100–2, 105, 107 (l), 108 (x 2), 109–10, 112 (x 2), 113, 116, 120, 122, 124 (x 2), 125–7, 136, 138–9, 142, 144–5, 147 and back cover, bottom two photographs: delphinium (*Delphinium elata*) and holly (*Ilex aquifolium*). CORALYN PASCALL, pp. 10, 19, 23, 26, 28 (l), 31, 34 (x 2), 36 (l), 37, 38 (l), 39, 41, 43, 45, 52 (x 2), 54 (r), 57 (r), 61, 63, 71, 79–80, 85, 93, 95–7, 98 (x 2), 103, 106, 107 (r), 111 (r), 117–18, 123, 129–32, 134, 137, 141, 143, 146 and back cover, top three photographs: guelder rose (*Viburnum opulus*); horse chestnut (*Aesculus hippocastanum*); foxglove (*Digitalis purpurea*). DAVE BEVAN, p. 84 (inset). ERIC SAWFORD, pp. 6–7, 8–9, 11, 15–17, 58–9, 65, 68, 70 (l), 72, 114–15 and 119. Cover, cutout front and back: elecampane (*Inula helenium*). FRANÇOIS GAIGNET, (front cover, main picture). GARDEN MATTERS, pp. 38, 86, 88 and 111 (l). HARRY SMITH HORTICULTURAL PHOTOGRAPHIC COLLECTION, pp. 18, 20–1, 24, 35, 56, 70 (r), 78, 84, 92, 94, 104, 133, 135, 140 and 147. JACQUES AMAND, p. 121. JOANNE COLLINS, p. 150. JULIAN SLATCHER, pp. 33, 49, 81, 82 and 113. ROYAL BOTANIC GARDENS, KEW, pp. 57 (inset), 64 (2 x inset), 69 (inset) and 145 (inset).

ABOUT THE AUTHOR

Catherine Collins started her career in horticulture when she left school, first working for her local parks department in Spelthorne, then moving on to the Royal Horticultural Society gardens at Wisley, in Surrey.

Catherine has worked in many areas of horticulture since, including soft landscaping and the hardy plants section of a garden centre in Shepperton, where she advised customers about plants and their aftercare. She has also been involved in adult education, running classes on various topics of gardening ranging from rock gardens to herbs and house plants. Catherine's pupils have included young students, newly-weds with their first garden, as well as experienced, retired students, from whom she learnt a thing or two as well.

Catherine recently moved to west Wales with her three children, to concentrate on writing and photography.

INDEX – BOTANICAL NAMES

INDEX OF COMMON NAMES

OTHER GARDENING TITLES
AVAILABLE FROM

GMC Publications

BOOKS

The above is a selection of the titles currently published or scheduled to be published.
All are available direct from the Publishers or through bookshops, newsagents and specialist retailers.
To place an order, or to obtain a complete catalogue covering all subjects, contact:

GMC Publications,
Castle Place, 166 High Street, Lewes, East Sussex BN7 1XU, United Kingdom
Tel: 01273 488005 Fax: 01273 478606
E-mail: pubs@thegmcgroup.com

Orders by credit card are accepted